FURS NOT MINE

Also by Andrea Cohen

The Cartographer's Vacation
Long Division
Kentucky Derby

FURS NOT MINE

Andrea Cohen

To Morie —
my FAVORITE
= 1
Russian.

Four Way Books
Tribeca

Much Love,
Andrea

for my mother

Please direct all inquiries to:
Editorial Office
Four Way Books
POB 535, Village Station
New York, NY 10014
www.fourwaybooks.com

Library of Congress Cataloging-in-Publication Data

Cohen, Andrea, [date]
[Poems. Selections]
Furs not mine / Andrea Cohen.
pages cm
ISBN 978-1-935536-51-2 (alk. paper)
I. Title.
PS3603.O3415F88 2015
811'.6—dc23

2014030212

This book is manufactured in the United States of America and printed on acid-free paper.

Four Way Books is a not-for-profit literary press. We are grateful for the assistance
we receive from individual donors, public arts agencies, and private foundations.

This publication is made possible with public funds from the National Endowment for the Arts

NYSCA

and from the New York State Council on the Arts, a state agency.

[clmp]

We are a proud member of the Council of Literary Magazines and Presses.

Distributed by University Press of New England
One Court Street, Lebanon, NH 03766

CONTENTS

The dream of green does not preclude new leaves.
　　　　　　　　　　　　　　　　—Reynolds Price

ONE

THE COMMITTEE WEIGHS IN

I tell my mother
I've won the Nobel Prize.

Again? she says. Which
discipline this time?

It's a little game
we play: I pretend

I'm somebody, she
pretends she isn't dead.

CLASP

You get used to it,
she said, meaning the delicate

mechanism of the diamond drop
passed on from her mother.

She was fastening the clasp
around my neck, meaning

preparing me for the fumbling
that inheritance presents, meaning

death. You get used to it, she
said, meaning being inserted

into the dark and learning to call
it something else—the way

of all flesh, for instance. It's
a box clasp: you slip a spring

into a box-like feature,
an 18th-century design modeled

after millennia of catches,
because the desire to hold

fast what we hold
dear is as old as sanity.

Great griefs are antidotes
for lesser sorrows. We patch

up loss with proverbs.
My hand goes absent-

mindedly to my throat,
as hers did, as her

mother's did, searching
out the tear-shaped

drop: I'm not gone yet.

CALENDAR

Some people, after the day
has passed, scratch an X

inside that box, as if
the past were a treasure

map and the sweet spot
for digging just missed.

Others, more hurried, employ
a slash-and-yearn policy,

their single diagonal
a ladder that showed up

too late for actual scrambling.
At the edge of known

physics, theorists like to say
days and minutes don't exist.

But calendars do: you can mass-
produce them with snapshots

of aspirations in Lisbon and Madrid.
In a pinch, in winter, they make

fine logs for the fire; in summer,
fans for shadeless expanses.

The fans burn too. Days are
like that: elastic and highly flammable.

WHOLE

Whole industries have sprung
from nothing, from someone
broken, crying: make me whole.

My brother, having broken
a green banana in half, held
the two snapped bits

up to my mother, who held
me in 1962 in the produce
section of the A&P, and holding

me (as yet unbroken), strolled, if
briefly, from my brother, pretending
not to know him, knowing his

inmost desire to be reunited
with a time before he knew me.
The cry insists: make me whole, as

if, made, we could be remade,
as if whole were a place
to point the golden Buick toward,

as if its station did not contain
chiefly the hole, the central O
of loss and going on.

BOILING POINT

Why should a watched
pot boil? It's busy
being watched, like

the child on the edge
of the high dive.
Why should she,

calling to her rapt
mother, *watch
me*, ever leap?

BREAKING AND ENTERING

The notion of the home
invasion is mostly myth.

Mostly we leave
ourselves unlocked, say

to a stranger: honey,
come on in.

Mostly the home
invasion is an inside

job: your interiors
get ravaged and pointing

a finger, you
mean to seek

damages. I left
the window open,

told the guard
dogs to roll over.

He pinched my last
candlesticks. If he'd

asked, I'd have filled
them with fire, I'd

have packed his candle-
lit supper to go, for the long,

sorry night he was entering.

22-FOOT MOTHER

The architect says: I want
a 22-foot mother. She's done

the calculations, considered
the engineering needed—given

her own dimensions—to install
herself comfortably, at 53,

inside her Übermother's lap.
In a pinch, she admits,

19 feet would do.
But she doesn't want

an average-size mother, doesn't crave
an average-size lap. The vastness

of her longing is evident
in the way she gazes

at anyone vacating chairs.
The exodus of laps

is endless and astonishing.
There is no consolation,

only lamentation, only going
back to the last drawing

board for 22 feet—
though 23 would be ideal.

EXODUS

The flat bread
that scratched

our throats
was not symbolic.

We left too quickly
to bring the symbols.

Neither did the bread
portend of manna.

It was bread.
We left

with the skin
on our backs,

with the imprint
of whips.

The symbols
came after,

finding us the way
a lost dog,

crossing deserts,
pinpoints the master

who can't
live without him.

INOPERABLE

Like all opposites, inoperable
comes from its root, from
the possible, in late

Latin, *operabilis*, in Latin,
operari, both of which sound
like something to sing about,

though it's worth noting
that opera makes unnatural
demands on the human instrument.

The natural inclination
of makers and what they make
is optimism, is believing the body

is not beyond repair, and labor
expended is not for naught, given
the possible positive outcome. Invasive

procedures are never the last
resort. The last place we visit
is the operating theater that shakes

its sorry head and signals, under
shuttered fluorescent lights,
under duress, *adieu.*

PASTORAL

Other people have
what they have.
She has the land.

She stands outside with it
all hours, all seasons.

She teaches it
survival skills: what
to do if food is scarce,

if lost or approached
by a stranger. She hides

from the pasture and takes
its picture in a blizzard,
in a drought, when, searching

the horizon for her, the land appears
most vulnerable, most unarranged.

That's the picture—not the one
grinning, with her, in sun—she'll
need, God forbid, should it

go missing. That's the photo
she'll plaster to utility poles,

to milk cartons: the likeness
of the pasture—bereft—
without her in it.

MASK

My mask has been recalled:
back to the factory it goes.

So too, my superhero
cape and the melancholy French

lullabies I was translating.
Soon there will be nothing

left of me but a glass
sigh, a wooden thigh,

and the love letters I send
religiously to myself,

the ones that come home
stamped: alas, unknown.

WISHFUL

After her last
breath I waited
for her next one.

It was weather for hearing
pins drop and morphine
drip. It had been

forecast. My father,
bedside, dropped the black
plastic comb he must

have been holding.
Shh, I scolded him,
thinking the ruckus

could wake her.

BIRDS WITH BLUE FEATHERS

Do you know the difference
between a bluebird
and a blue jay?

Yes, I say.
What is it? he asks.
How cruel for the blue jay

to demand proof.
He's made sure I've never
seen the rare bluebird

of happiness, not
even in a picture book.
They're both blue,

I say. One stands
for happiness,
the other one is you.

BRUTAL

Brutal to give
the prisoner a window—
a blue sky glimpse—

as if an afterlife
existed. Brutal
for you to parade

in a body
in the same
room where I dream you.

THE CARE AND FEEDING OF ONE-WAY MIRRORS

Do not overfeed either
side of the mirror. Do not
assume that the man brought in

for questioning does not
intuit you observing.
At regular intervals, the observer

and the observed, also known
as the suspect and the one
who suspects him, should

trade places. All cases
involving one-way mirrors
require this balance, which

appears foolish only until a bare
bulb dangles above you, until
staring long enough at yourself

in the glass, even you
doubt the airtight alibi
you keep repeating.

PALL

It contains all,
but you knew that,

and how it falls
over everything,

then asks
those so bereft

they can barely
stand to stand

tall, to bear
it onward.

THE IMAGINARY FURROW I WAS PLOWING

for Anna Schuleit Haber

The imaginary furrow I was plowing
was no less real than the invisible

ropes harnessed to the invisible
plow, nor less real than the heavens

and its beings watching me, nor the scarlet
and purple confetti wheeling out from me

into the imaginary furrow I was plowing.
I have always tilled the earth

of the imagined, beside my brethren
similarly yoked; this was my calling,

and never easy beneath the heavens
unblinking and the muted enthusiasm

of those who called me *patient.* They
called themselves, *doctor, orderly, nurse,*

my *next of kin*: those not harnessed
to the invisible, those not locked

into it, had no relation to me. I pitied
them, but there was little

time for pity, given my plow to guide,
given the essential furrow I seeded.

WE LOST OUR EVERYTHING

We lost our everything,
she said, which said everything
about loss. My accumulation
dictates my ruin; it's different

from your dismantling, which
can happen slowly or all at once.
What's crucial is a total
inventory, which may reveal

some one element not obliterated.
We lost our everything,
she said—*we*—she repeated,
meaning the we-ness remained,

which in the end must be the seed
of re-beginning, the seed that
divines the plow, the ounce
of dirt, the memory of digging.

BLUE

You see them gearing
up: the young
in their new uniforms.

Eschewing what we
stood for (hid from),
refusing to call themselves

warriors or peacekeepers,
they've ditched the jigsaw
of jungle and desert, choosing

a blue that suggests
they mean business, meaning
to camouflage themselves in sky.

They're the ultimate in fly
guys and gals—indistinguishable
from some bright day. Theirs

is a nuanced frontier; they're
saying *no thanks* to the front,
to no man's land, to take

no prisoners. Already I'm seeing
fewer and fewer of these
Houdinis—kids really—and I

can't—visoring my upward
gaze—not salute them,
not mouth *Godspeed.*

MACAROONS

I get it now.
You're dead.
You can't do
everything
you used to.
Reruns instead
of new episodes.
I get it.
You can't send
macaroons this Passover,
those dense confections
without flour, conforming
to the rules
of kashrut, the rules
of engagement, which
in the case of our people,
involved fleeing, trading
slavery for the desert.
The land of milk & honey
was a kind of paint-
by-numbers kit
everybody lugged
in his head through
sandy ditches. It's
best not to commit
directions to Nirvana
to paper: they could be
stolen or confiscated, or
worse: the place itself
obliterated. Forty
years is a long time

to get where you're going.
Where are you promised?
In the end you spoke
of a boat ride, of
booking passage second-
class, on a vessel that lacked
a rudder, an engine, a sail.
Kaput, you said.
You were looking
for a solution.
Why now? someone
asked—less question
than demand. You
had to go. I
get it. We prepped
you for a journey,
because the mind
gets stuck on the speed
bumps of *fin*, of *finito*.
The mind insists
on one more
road, one more hello.
I get it: you won't
be posting macaroons
this year. No problem,
Mom. Just send the recipe.

BARGAIN

We paid him next
to nothing—less than the little
he'd asked for—to lead us

at dusk from the pyramids
on camels into the desert.
Such slim wages

to take us, without
complaint, all that way—
so far, without a star.

We were in the middle
of nowhere, or at its edge.
Friends, he asked, from

inside that blackness,
what will you pay me
to take you back?

BRICKS

Beside the most
humble abode—

think one window,
think one flimsy door—

a stash of bricks
is neatly piled, the building

blocks for some addition,
which, in the mind

of the will-be builder,
figures as second bedroom

one year, as kitchen
the next. The solidity

of bricks shape-
shifts easily and will not

be upstaged by famine,
by locusts, by the run

of bad luck that suns
itself nearby. Sometimes

the pile will be guarded
by a thin dog or by chain link,

sometimes disguised
by the flapping of a tarp

cobalt as ocean, as the big
sky idea it is: a kind of spire

in training, patient
to be built, whispering

blueprints nightly, as lullaby,
as come hither, inside

the harshest winds
to its steadfast architect.

AND

And in the beginning, he liked
to begin his bedtime stories, implying

a back story to every story, an antechamber
to the official commencement, and the story

was always stocked with A begetting B, and C
begetting D, and so on and repeating, people

peopling the earth, and miracles and woes—
locusts, floods, rainbows, the burning bush—

overlapping, infidels turning to salt and
prophets turning over a new joy and a grief and

when we'd get to the end of the book we'd begin
again and it seemed we were a wheel and

we kept the story going and I believed and I had
faith that as long as we could keep going back

to the garden it would be morning and evening and
despite the serpent and the dark and twisting

turns, it would be good—

SWALLOW

Sometimes you've got, he
said, to swallow the bullet.
I guess you do that

when you're out of bitter
pills, when you're under
enemy fire, without benefit

of anesthesia, when the bullet
you've been biting could
be used against you.

THE WAGES OF PEACE

I miss
my enemy.

My rifle misses
aiming and missing.

My trigger finger,
triggerless, isn't happy.

Hapless, it busies
itself, fingering

cheery photos
of my dead.

I'm there
among them.

I'm walking
beside my shoes.

It was a mistake
to kill my enemy,

a tactical error, short-
sighted. What can I

do now, but send my widow
to his, begging forgiveness?

THE GOOD AND THE BAD

In dreams my dead spill
popcorn at the opera, they

guffaw at the death scenes.
My mother tells me to let

the ants in my ant farm go.
When we went mano-

a-mano in the flesh,
I never listened. But

in these dreamed cameos,
I let the ants go, which

surprises, then saddens
my mother, as if she

grasps that the price of being
dreamed is to keep vanishing.

CLIFFSIDE

At the Wicked Oyster, I
sit between Lou, who
builds seawalls, and Hugh,
who used to. Between
them is an encyclopedia
of hard engineering, of rubble
mounds and concrete armor.
We're sitting at the bar,
which is what people
without other people
do. Hugh drinks Coke,
Lou cozies his beer in foam.
They agree that static
features conflict with nature.
Once your neighbor builds,
you've got to build too,
because waves insist
on taking: it's a system
of accretion and loss.
They know that, their backs
and backhoes having
shifted mountains.
A finger in the dike,
Hugh says. Lou nods.
I'm trying to read
an article on grief. My
whiskey leaks into *trigger*,
into *time*. Today, cliffside,
I realized what fundamental
trade death makes: in lieu
of you, the memory of you.

Not fair, I'd say. Life
isn't, you said, or rather,
the memory of you
spoke, and wave upon
wave keeps repeating.

LATE ROSES, 1959

after Josef Sudek

The glass of water
was thirsty. I gave it
three roses on one
stem and stood it

by the window.
Outside there was a tree.
Rain streaked the window.
A nautilus shell sat

by the glass. You could tell
the shell and the roses
hoped the rain would stop,
hoped that their interior

lives would end, that
they'd get to play
with the other shells,
the other roses.

It goes without saying
that they'd miss
the glass of water,
that they'd send it a letter.

ON AN OPERA IN PROGRESS

after Aleksandra Vrebalov

Loneliness is systemic.
Is this my warning
to those children?

I hear their voices
at play but can't
see them and vice versa.

That may be best:
let them go on
shepherding the past.

Don't distract them
with the rumbling
advance, with the tanks

whose path is inevitable.
You, who have yet
to grunt and grin your way

forward, you unborn
to ache or joy, what
red flag would you

sense, what siren sound?
Don't fret: all is lost
and revealed. Snow falls

on your behalf. It quiets
the forest, it invites
children, racing through

the village, to be children.

STICK FIGURE

Children comprehend
the need for speed,
rendering torso and limbs

with Morse code dashes,
the balloon head
a hurried zero.

If there's time,
the child sketches
a bent twig as smile,

if not on the face,
nearby, like a stick
the optimistic dog runs after.

FURS NOT MINE

The Russians have a way of saying
what must be said, and one

need not be or speak Russian
to comprehend the sense

of furs not mine. One need only
to have known deep cold, an inmost

Siberia made more Siberian by one
who basks nearby, oblivious in her Bolivia.

TWO

MOMENT OF TRUTH

A matador imagines he has
many moments of truth, those

moments before his final sword
play, before he and the bull part ways.

Then one evening, in the sky
above the arena, he sees a reddish-

yellow streak that mimics his cape,
and a cloud that mirrors

his likeness precisely. It's a momentary
distraction above the crowd

that calls for blood, as the bull
is upon him. This is the critical

moment for the toreador: seeing
the airy man he might have been.

RIDDLE

It pleased my brother
to trip me up.

Which weighs more: pound
of nails or pound of feathers?

After crossing the heather
several times, nearly mad

in mad weather, I comprehend
that the expression—

all things being equal—
is fairy tale and old wives' story.

X never equals Y.
Moreover, X doesn't even,

in X, find its equivalent.
In the basement, my father

sorts bright common nails,
by size, by degree of rust,

into mason jars whose lids he's nailed
to the ceiling for safe-keeping.

With nothing left
to build, we mend.

Upstairs I caress
my dead mother's boa,

an over-the-top accoutrement,
still sandalwood-scented, an extravagance

like the flight of geese last
spring, when I couldn't

know: not nails, but feathers.

THE BONES OF THE INNER EAR

after David Shrigley

The bones of the inner ear
caught in the cannibal's throat—

what do they hear or comprehend?
Do they speculate that the cannibal,

gasping, asks for forgiveness?
Are the bones of the inner ear, flesh-

stripped, deaf to such pleas?
Or do they listen?

Are they moved, in the cannibal's throat,
in a last blast of mercy to collapse?

SELF PORTRAIT AS A DROWNING MAN

Dieter Roth painted himself
and cut the painting into bits.
Some cutters cut

to see blood flow, to feel
light-headed and alive.
Cutting, for such people,

is constructive. They shape
who they are as a child
from construction paper makes

a paper doll. Some people
feel an arm or leg
doesn't belong to them.

They get fifth or sixth
opinions until a physician
agrees to cut it off. Dieter

Roth cut himself
into pieces to fit
inside a suitcase. To

make a drowning man,
take all his fragments
and add water.

PROGRESS REPORT SEPTEMBER 2010

My father's lifted 25.8
African elephants, or rather,
their equivalent, at the gym.
African elephants are larger
than Asian elephants and use
their tusks for digging
roots, for stripping bark
from baobab trees, for fighting
the competition come
mating season. This
is the second season
of autumn since my father
stopped lifting my mother,
in mock exhaustion, over
the threshold. There are two
types of elephants and two
sorts of my father: one
companioned by my mother, one
by her ghost. One went
to the gym to lift weights daily;
the other goes now in his place.
25.8 African elephants
isn't bad for a man
at 82, in the category
of lifting, but what
the progress report omits
is the more difficult, the less
showy side of pumping iron:
the lowering of 25.8
African elephants, that awkward,
grunting feat which my father's mathematical

brain—his head now bent
on subtraction—translates into
1588.3 repetitions of giving
my mother back to the earth.
Of course, September progress reports
mean to be uplifting, mean to make
Dad Atlas on the Serengeti.
But the old souls of 25.8 African elephants
sense his sense of a weight he can't
put down, and the savannah from
which they've been banished. How
regal and imperiled the apparitions,
dragging their sad tusks
across the red dust of our suburbia.

THEORY OF THE BROKEN

The theory of the broken
window is that breakage

is a temporary state.
The theory states

that one window,
fixed, opens up

a window for renewal.
The repair of windows

is twofold: insert
the glass into the frame,

then institute a buyback
plan: for every stone

about to be thrown, a glass
of milk, a bedtime glory.

AFTER CATULLUS

Brother, we've lost
the same home.
Walls still stand,
but the scent
that made us
has crept off.

BRIDGE

after Su Tung-P'o (for Yotam Haber)

Write to me, he said,
when you reach the final bridge.

But how could I know
which bridge was the last?

I was a girl and this my first river.
There was a moon to consider.

There were reeds and swells and boys
who rippled in from both shores.

At last I wrecked
the leaf that was my boat.

I wrote to him:
Come. I've had enough of bridges.

PARTIAL RECIPE FOR BRUNSWICK STEW

Ground beef in enough water
to cover. Simmer. Add canned

tomatoes, lima beans, corn and celery,
Tabasco, onion, bell pepper. That's what

the dead do: leave us
with a list of ingredients, with

meager instruction, without
measurements. This is the partial

recipe, penciled in my mother's hand,
on a child's scrap of red and blue

ruled paper. There are no
rules for bringing up

the rear: only hunger
and the fiery memory

of the bowl we believed
could never be empty.

COMPASS

It's easy, being
gloved in a mild

clime, finding one lamb-
skin mitten, to place

it ostentatiously
on a gatepost

for its owner.
Less straightforward

is the ascent
in a blizzard: coming

upon the single
lamb, one struggles

with hunger and cold
truths, with the balancing

act high ground presents.

BOMB

English is hard
to explain. Why
is one *b* loud

and one silent?
Why does one
house stand

and another crumble?
Why does one
mother, falling

on the open
wound of her one
son, howl,

while another
opens her mouth
and goes dumb?

ON BLUEBERRY PICKING

Mostly it consists of pretending
not to pick them, since the wild bush—
more a tree really, thrives in plain
view among scrub pines, along the road
that leads to the Truro sea. So when cars
near, we turn from the bush, busying
our hands in air, as if plucking a thread
of conversation started ages back—
which, between my mother and me,
must be the case. When a car gets far
enough away, we resume our harvest:
hands and lips stained with what
the season tenders: the fat or compact
berries that will never be sweeter than
this moment. I say this in the present
tense, as if the harvesting goes on.
I recall my mother doubled over
in laughter, midsummer, by that bush,
and a man in a blue truck stopping.
I'm a doctor, he said. *Are you ill?*
Physicians are trained to see what's
amiss, what they might fix. Bliss,
from a distance, can look like pain.
But it was bliss, I'm thinking now,
speeding past all those ghosts in flower.

POCO

Do you speak Spanish? someone
asks my father. Poco, he says,
which is his one word in Spanish, which

opens the floodgates because "a little"
is open to interpretation.
My little might be microscopic

beside yours. His little won't admit
how little he understands, how
little he is comprehended.

His little says: let's pretend
we come from the same planet,
that similar suns and moons

and deaths arrange us. His poco says
to the señorita: Haven't we met?
And to the bricklayer: Aren't we birds

of a feather? His poco says:
my little may be the rind, but it's part
of the orange, and it's mine. More

tequila? More beans? More sightseeing?
the bartender, the waitress, the tour
guide ask. Poco, my father says, meaning

as much as we can, meaning,
please, meaning keep the river
cascading, the nada at bay.

MEANS OF TRANSPORT

I'm a streetcar
slowing: my mother

steps off and my
dead step on.

This goes on
and on until

I'm a streetcar
no longer: I'm

my mother,
stepping off—

THREE

EXPLANATION (HIROSHIMA)

You have to explain
to the new girl, you

always do, to the one
who means, staying late,

to scrub the stain
from the marble stair

displayed at the museum.
You have to explain

that the darkness is not
a stain she can erase.

Rather, it's shade
and shadow, a stranglehold

that's all that's left
of a girl and boy who

sat on the school stair
as children do, and vanished.

You have to explain:
we guard the stain.

IMPRISONED BY THE PAST

She sat down in it.
There was barely
room to stand. She

could hear people
not under lock and key
beseeching: dig

your way out. How
little they comprehended.
All she had, imprisoned

by the past, was a sad,
plastic spoon and all those
ghosts in need of feeding.

TENDER

Unfolded, crisp–here
are your dollars, with
interest, with blood

and sweat, with
antiseptic and the elbow
grease that couldn't

quite clean them. Here
are your dollars, with
their dead men, with their

flags, with their pyramids
chiseled and eagles flattened.
Give me back my hours.

THIS ICARUS

As in every version, there's a boy
who flies too high, a father, and too many questions.
How did Icarus, sixteen, sneak past security

at Charlotte Douglas International Airport?
How did he secret himself inside the wheel well

of a Boeing 737, and what was Icarus thinking?
A happy boy is how his father describes him,
though happiness is not incompatible

with a desire to fly too high.
The boy's brother suggests unrest,

disaffection. At that age, does
one fly more likely toward or from?
Why, Icarus, the wheel well? He left

a greasy handprint there, a stain
his father longs to place his hand

inside, though he can't bring himself
to envision his son, curled, in red jersey
and black sneakers inside that chamber, sub-zero.

A detective says the boy's death
would have been quick and painless,

though a pilot overheard describes
how the wheel, retracting after take-off,
would have crushed Icarus, whose father

can't go there. Instead, he goes
to his son's room, to the bedside

book with this line highlighted:
Love the questions. The father of Icarus
does not love them. He loves his son,

with whom he flew one Independence
night up the Eastern Seaboard, a feast

of fireworks beneath them. He thinks
of Icarus staring down the wheel well.
How? Why? Once a boy gets flight

without a flight plan in his head,
all bets are off. The autopsy showed

trauma consistent with freefalling.
His father keeps the boy's room
as it was: shrine to the afternoon

before he flew, before he fell,
before the father held the slender

book of Rilke, the book of letters,
before his son was a locked room,
ledger in a foreign tongue.

PHOEBE

Me two, I hear,
then paired convert

her two notes
to *we three.*

Addition, then
subtraction: *why*

me? the phoebe
sings upon my

loss, and then
another spring,

winging from the mud
cup of last year's nest:

repeat, repeat, repeat.

FRANK O'HARA'S GOLDEN GONDOLA

It never really belonged
to Frank, or should I say,
Mr. O'Hara. He stashed it
in the pocket of his white
linen jacket after bantering, after
buying the trinket from a merchant
of gilded kitsch on the Rialto,
and presented it, not
to his lover, Bill, but to
his young friend Lise, as the three
drifted in a larger golden gondola
beneath the Bridge of Sighs. She
was the daughter of a painter
Frank was not. Like her father,
she liked Frank a lot, but more
than Frank, she adored Bill, his lover, and held
out hope that Frank's gift beneath
the Bridge of Sighs signified a rift
between Bill and Frank, a narrows
through which she and Bill might
slip into Venetian bliss. A girl,
at ten, dreams like this. She considers
everything, the way Frank O'Hara did
in his lunchtime walks, in "The Day Lady Died."
While Lise and Bill and Frank, guided
by a lithe gondolier making eyes
at Frank and Bill, drifted down
the canal, Frank would have mentioned
Byron, how he coined the phrase,
The Bridge of Sighs, imagining the convicts,
prison-led, getting their last glimpse

of the City of Masks. In fact,
Venice was visible from the prison, which
must have tormented the prisoners more,
the way it's torture to ride in a gondola
with your secret love nuzzling his lover.
The girl of ten lugged the golden gondola
across the years of rooms until a roommate
in Key West pilfered it, and the gondola
with its flaking, gold paint got passed
like a party girl from stranger to stranger,
enlisted as paper weight, as door stop, as
the blunt instrument a memento
of the City of Bridges, cast out, becomes.

HUBCAP

Not even his own
hubcap is how the newscast
described what he was after,
crossing three lanes of highway
to the grassy median. Retrieving,
they said, which is not inaccurate,
since desire made the hubcap
his, the way longing constructs
every part of us. He didn't even
own a car, his stunned son said,
on camera, unshaven, after
the hit-and-run, though the son
would have only known parts
of his father, might not have
been privy to the Sunday ritual
of scouting out discarded or lost
bits, meaning to build his dream
vehicle from scrap. A hairdresser
the son never met shows
up at the service and says:
your father had a beautiful head
of dreams and asks: was the hubcap
a '73 Mercury? That's what he needed.
The son says: he didn't even
know how to drive. The newscast
pans from passing cars to the grassy
median, back and forth, as in
a tennis match. A witness says that after
he grabbed the hubcap, he leapt,
as a tennis victor will, across the net,
but into traffic. The son nods:

his father loved tennis once, or loved
nodding his head from side
to side, a gesture that seemed
like *no* to those who didn't know him.
Now the son numbers himself
among them, thinks his father
was scanning left and right for the glint
of a hubcap he could hammer out,
for a door panel or chrome handle,
flashes of the getaway car
the stalled man imagines.

SINS OF OMISSION

It's not God
we're putting out
I tell my son
when we're putting
the wreath out
with the trash—
though God knows
we've been left
out by God.
The last part I
say under my breath
so my son
won't hear. But—
little pitchers—he
does. Mom, he
says, his brow knit.
It's the moment
I've dreaded. You
know I don't
really exist, right?
I breathe, I
stay calm. Let's
talk about it, I say,
thinking of the family
tree shivering in winter.
But already he's taken
the dream he
is into the forest
of his room

to ruminate on
all the shapes
he'll never take.

CHERRIES

In the minute it took
to fetch the blue bowl

from the kitchen
to pick the just-ripe

cherries, the blackbirds
had come. They picked

the branches clean, ascending
into their own blue bowl.

Lacking wings, I
scan for meaning.

We were all hungry.
We were all fed.

PEACHES OCCUR

Peaches occur in a range
of colors not readily
described as peach.
It's peachy to think this

isn't the case, that peaches
resist the complication, say,
of apples, which come
with all that baggage. If

the peach could simply be
a peach, you wouldn't see
the shy girl caressing
the fuzz as if it was

what it isn't. It isn't
easy hanging low, being
ripe for picking. Someone
bites into your prime time and

wham—an explosion of home-
made cobbler, of sisters and brothers,
of peach brandy in tumblers, a mother,
a father, peach jam, peach pie, every

sweetness a peach can utter at the long-
gone kitchen table, in a summer
resurrected. The past occurs
in a range of shades not

readily described as past. Fulvous
describes the reddish-yellow
of some peaches, of some
singular and setting sun.

PREMIUM, DUSK

My mother paid six cents
for every jar of fireflies.

She paid an extra cent
for every hole drilled in the lid.

But the highest fee went
to the empty jar, the jar

around which the fireflies
flashed their ecstasies,

around which we'd sit
and sing as if

around a campfire.
You could only sit

so close, given
the glow, given

the sparks, which,
given, fever my cheek still.

INSTRUCTIONS FOR MY FUNERAL

I have but one
request: serve chocolate-
dipped crickets; this should be
an event no one
will wish to repeat.
In addition, waive all
admission fees, blast
rockabilly from one speaker,
Bach from the quartet.
Let the dress code
be optional, or hiphop.
Don't scrimp when it comes
to cloud-seeding. Seat
the starlets near
the tear buckets, give
the bartenders stiff ones
before they report,
let them serve ether
cocktails and please do
trouble yourself enough
to fetch my mother
back from the hereafter—
expenses be damned! I'll
need her to hold my hand.
And lastly, friend, crack
the lid a little, enough
to confirm a casket
of mistaken identity.
Tell the sad sack inside,
better luck next time. Tell

my mother, as long
as she's here, to
linger for the festivities.

ITALIAN GUARD DOGS OF PETERBOROUGH

The Italian guard dogs of Peterborough guard
sheep, and if you're me, one of the three
Maremmas will catapult himself between the wires
of an electrified fence to escort you past his pasture.
Next week, a borrowed dog, a shepherd,
will lead the sheep and lambs across the street
to another pasture. It's easier getting the sheep
to buy into decampment. They've made
the crossing before, whereas the lambs haven't
and lambs are skeptical of migration, and rightly so.
There's considerable history of going
like a lamb, but the lambs need to go
and come back because it turns out
you can only live in your own crap
for nine weeks before the parasites get nasty.
But that's not the point. The point
is Aldo, the point dog who sidles up
to me because, in addition to guarding sheep
and lambs, an Italian guard dog guards
his future. He does this as we all do: by
dreaming of expansion. His flexing in my direction
is how Aldo applies for the select position
of guarding me, and though accustomed to living
outdoors, in mud and blizzards, Aldo retains
the regal countenance that is his birthright.
He ambles like an Italian god beside me,
the length of the electric fence. No hard
sell here, just the demonstration of jumping
through fire on my behalf, providing an inkling
of what being guarded by Aldo might feel like.
It feels good. I'm wondering what I'd need

to give up to be guarded by Aldo when his owner
and handler, an eager, petite woman
named Frances, rushes toward us with a choke chain
and an apology—the former for Aldo, the latter
for me. Clearly, she and Aldo have not discussed
his plans for expansion. But Frances discusses much
with me: how she grew up in Turkey, the daughter
of missionaries, which explains her tendency
toward flocks, and how she's moved from pasture
to pasture, from California to Durango to Maine,
where she cared for Phyllis Wyeth, whose accident
happened when she was still a Dupont.
If only she'd had an Italian guard dog!
Frances and her husband got the Maremmas
because the coyotes were getting the sheep, despite
the best efforts of the guard donkey, since retired.
Behind the L of the farmhouse, Frances shows me
where the pasture drops off imperceptibly, hemmed
in by a hidden stone wall that keeps the sheep below
but lets the eye graze continuously. It's genius, this
bit of British landscaping and it must be what
it feels like to be guarded by Aldo—walled
in, without knowing. I'm guessing that my favorite
Maremma, back with his sheep now, is inking
a contract for me to consider. The terms would be favorable
for Aldo, for me: a win-win scenario at half or twice the price.
Frances explains the complicated lineage of the dogs,
how she breeds but won't sell them to anyone who can't
pronounce Maremma properly: like the mare
that comes before an Emma. Aldo is less concerned
with pronunciation: he's a cloud summoned

82

to earth and he means to stay busy, to ensure
that the guard dogs who report to him aren't idle either.
Frances shows me an allée of grass close to the house,
where the road once ran before a deadly turn
further east caused them to move it. Aldo must
sense that legacy of risk and loss: Italian guard dogs
have long memories and a far better attention span
than I, and by the way, Francis tells me
they keep their Bugattis in the barn. Bugattis. Plural.
These are another kind of Italian guard dog. They
guard the goddesses of opulence and speed and La Dolce Vita.
We drive them, Frances admits, sheepishly,
in the rallies. It's elitist, but we like it.
I'm invited to return soon, when her husband
will introduce me to the Bugattis. I think I will
dress for the occasion, maybe even wear a shirt,
or a shirt with a collar. I should come
with an answer for Aldo, too, who is too
proud to beg. Instead, splendidly he patrols
his side of the fence, in a town founded in 1760
by Italian guard dogs, a hamlet that relies on stealth
protection, fortressing its borders with a sign that reads:
Peterborough A Good Town to Live In—a greeting
humble enough to defend against fatal flaws
such as hubris or too much tourism. I will return
with an answer for the Italian guard dogs of Peterborough—
three clouds beneath a cloudless sky.

ENGLISH AS THIRD LANGUAGE

Burly and squat, he stood
in full sun and Russian

accent beside the river,
his arms outstretched,

his shoulders a perch
for pigeons and wrens.

As for telltale crumbs,
there were none. He

shrugged—a loaf
of a man: *I am, they come.*

LET ME DIE IN MADRID

Let me die in Madrid
when the grave diggers
are on strike. Let the drivers

of buses, in sympathy, strike
too, keeping my three paid
mourners, who might have crossed

picket lines, from reaching the cemetery.
Let one daring municipal clerk,
in support of the grave diggers

and the drivers of buses and all
of us who believe we deserve
a tiny bit more, mark *clerical*

error on my death certificate.
Let me stand at my favorite
spot at my favorite corner bar,

let me raise an empty glass
to the empty graves, empty buses,
empty pockets of my unpaid mourners.

MEMORY FOAM

Why stop there?
I want memory

underwear and a memory
chair. The stair

should be a memory
stair, wherever I

appear should remember
me, and you, when

we first meet, since
you've been laboring—

I guess—like the rest
of us, as a memory

apprentice, can step
inside my undulations.

Come, remind me
why we bend.

INVENTION OF GRIEF

I give it fur
and six hind legs.
I give it one
month to live,
a glass eye,
a bed of grass.
One by one,
grief chews its six
feet off. It scans
the room and with
a voice I never
gave exclaims: a glass
room, cool! Grief
tramples its grass
bed into a cozy
nest. Who taught
grief that? It's wild
antecedents: happiness
and sans souci.

FIRST THOUGHT, BEST THOUGHT

I'm three or four,
hidden in the branches

of the cherry tree.
I don't ask: how

did I get here?
I don't fear falling.

The job of the blossom
is to bloom, to be

beautifully unschooled in ruin.

GRAVY BOAT

I've got one foot
in the gravy, one
in the gravy boat.

It's the same foot.
The other one?
I cut it off.

Otherwise it would
have stood its one
foot in the grave.

I balance easily now
in the gravy boat
on my good foot.

I got the boat cheap,
when Bolivia lost its coast
and auctioned off its navy.

Where am I sailing?
Who can say?
Goodbye Bolivia, hello gravy!

This is what depression feels like:

— a sudden rocket launch,
~~, the clust~~

If you were chloroformed
in your bed,
hauled to a rocket, ~~strapped in~~,
carelessly, the workmen smoking
and checking launch times,
and if they'll have time to grab
a Dunkin before.

if you were launched, woke up
just in time to feel the earth drop,
and felt ~~the~~ it smaller smaller smaller
~~if you were~~ and after a week nothing much
around you anymore.
All the food tastes like astronaut food.
You have to lift weights to survive to
your bones dont thin + break + bury you.
You forget time of day or years.
And if your mother calls,
and asks when you are coming over
you try so hard to pretend that you are
just down the street,
when as your tears fill up the weightlessness,
"I ~~dont~~ ~~know,~~ ~~mom.~~
I ~~do it~~ ~~know~~" maybe tomorrow,
maybe."

ACKNOWLEDGMENTS

I am grateful to the editors of the following journals in which these poems first appeared, sometimes in slightly different incarnations:

The Atlantic Monthly, The Cincinnati Review, Consequence, Diode, Front Porch Journal, Gastronomica, Gwarlingo, Harvard Divinity Bulletin, The Hudson Review, Ibbetson Street, Journal of Family Life, Mind & Life, The New Republic, Orion, Plume, Poetry, Salamander, Sixth Finch, Smartish Pace, The Tablet, Terrrain, The Threepenny Review, Thrush, Upstreet, Verse Daily, and *Women's Voices for Change.*

Lamplighters, all: Francesca Bewer, Gail Mazur, Amy Anderson, Anna Schuleit Haber, Giavanna Munafo, Gail Caldwell, Rebecca Morgan Frank, Jennifer Clarvoe, Bob Hicok, and my family. Thanks to Martha Rhodes at Four Way, and picnic baskets to The MacDowell Colony and all its tenders. And Naomi Wallace, you rock.

Grief is inconvenient.
I want to make a schedull
to shut you in: one hour a week
we will sit and you can air
your grievances.
I'll make a special costume for it,
   fast before and after.

But you are ill-mannered.
You barge in on the T,
   on the phone,

Andrea Cohen's poems and stories have appeared in *The Atlantic Monthly*, *The New Republic*, *The New Yorker*, *Poetry*, *The Threepenny Review*, and elsewhere. Her previous poetry collections include *The Cartographer's Vacation*, winner of the Owl Creek Poetry Prize, *Long Division*, and *Kentucky Derby*. She has received a PEN Discovery Award, *Glimmer Train's* Short Fiction Award, and several residencies at The MacDowell Colony. She directs the Blacksmith House Poetry Series in Cambridge, Massachusetts, and the Writers House at Merrimack College.

Publication of this book was made possible by grants and donations. We are also grateful to those individuals who participated in our 2014 Build a Book Program. They are:

Nickie Albert
Michele Albright
Whitney Armstrong
Jan Bender-Zanoni
Juanita Brunk
Ryan George
Michelle Gillett
Elizabeth Green
Dr. Lauri Grossman
Martin Haugh
Nathaniel Hutner
Lee Jenkins
Ryan Johnson
Joy Katz
Neal Kawesch
Brett Fletcher Lauer & Gretchen Scott
David Lee
Daniel Levin
Howard Levy
Owen Lewis
Paul Lisicky
Maija Makinen
Aubrie Marrin
Malia Mason
Catherine McArthur
Nathan McClain
Michael Morse
Chessy Normile
Rebecca Okrent
Eileen Pollack

Barbara Preminger
Kevin Prufer
Soraya Shalforoosh
Alice St. Claire-Long
Megan Staffel
Marjorie & Lew Tesser
Boris Thomas
William Wenthe